Original title:
Beneath the Orange Tree

Copyright © 2025 Creative Arts Management OÜ
All rights reserved.

Author: Hugo Fitzgerald
ISBN HARDBACK: 978-1-80586-297-0
ISBN PAPERBACK: 978-1-80586-769-2

Recollections Under Tangy Umbrellas

Under vibrant branches, shadows play,
Lemons drop like laughter, bright and gay.
We chase the squirrels, they steal our snacks,
A citrus party, with no time to relax.

The breeze is teasing, a zesty breeze,
Limes whisper jokes, putting minds at ease.
We throw the peels, a slippery mess,
In this fruity realm, we wear our zest.

The Citrus Canopy Chronicles

In a world of zest, where tangy dreams grow,
Grapefruits gossip in a cheery flow.
We dance with oranges, all dressed in peels,
Laughter echoes, like juicy meals.

A tangerine fell, right on my head,
You'd think it was planned, my face turned red.
But giggles erupted, like juice it spilled,\nUnder this canopy, we all feel thrilled.

Lament of the Falling Fruit

Entangled in laughter, we watched them drop,
A tangerine tango, it just won't stop.
The fruits are plotting, a fruity descent,
As we dodge their antics, what a sad event!

The ground is a carpet of citrus delight,
If you slip and slide, it's a comical sight.
We bemoan the oranges, so bold and free,
Their reckless abandon, oh, the irony!

Portrait of a Sunlit Retreat

In the sunlit refuge, where sweetness abounds,
Grapes giggle softly, in whispered sounds.
A hammock sways, like a juicy dream,
Snapshots of fun, life's refreshing theme.

With each sip of tang, we toast to the skies,
Under this dazzling, fruity disguise.
Mirth overflows, like juice from a squeeze,
In this whimsical garden, we'll never cease.

Luminous Canopies of Delight

In a world where shadows play,
Laughter dances in the sway.
Squirrels plotting cheeky steals,
Orange dreams and fruity meals.

Beneath the sun's warm, glowing gleam,
We've launched a citrus-based dream.
Giggles echo, bouncing light,
As oranges roll, what a sight!

Orange Light through Twisted Boughs

Twisted branches, what a scene,
A fruit-filled jungle, oh so keen!
Chasing shadows, tripping small,
Watch those oranges, they might fall!

With a wink, and a little twist,
A clumsy dance that can't be missed.
The juice may splash, it's all in fun,
Under this canopy, we run!

Orchard Reveries at Dusk

As the sun dips low, we roam,
Oranges glow, their vibrant foam.
Whispers of fruit, secrets abound,
In twilight's charm, joy's unbound.

A mischievous grin, a playful chat,
Oranges giggle, imagine that!
The dusk wraps us in citrus dreams,
In this orchard, laughter beams!

The Dance of Ripening Fruit

Ripening treasures, what a tease,
They jive and jiggle, with the breeze.
A fruit fiesta, oh what fun,
Watch them shimmy, one by one!

With every sway, the laughter spreads,
As fruity waltzes fill our heads.
In this orchard, joy's the root,
Come join the dance, let's shake the fruit!

The Light That Filters Through

In the glare of a sunbeam's dance,
I found my shoe, lost in a prance.
The colors shift, in shadows they tease,
While squirrels plot in their silly degrees.

A bird tries to sing, but sneezes instead,
While ants carry crumbs to a mighty bread.
The laughter flows like honey on toast,
In this whimsical world, I love the most.

Sunkissed Memories of Innocence

We'd chase our shadows on golden grass,
With lemonade dreams that never pass.
Jumping in puddles, splashing with glee,
Sticking our tongues out for the sweet bee.

Predicting the weather with dandelion fluff,
We'd race the clouds, bluffing our tough.
With popsicle smiles and sticky hands,
Our giggles were music in sun-soaked lands.

Echoes of Days Gone By

Old swings creak tales of days reveling bright,
Where time wore laughter, morning till night.
We'd climb the fence, our secret domain,
In a world where only giggles remain.

The ice cream truck's jingle, a siren's call,
As we raced to the curb, pretending to fall.
Our bellies were full, but we'd still take one scoop,
In our kingdom of fun, we'd always regroup.

The Stillness Between the Leaves

In dappled shade, the chatter's a buzz,
As butterflies dance, with giggles that fuzz.
The branches sway gently, a playful tease,
Crickets conduct the symphony with ease.

We'd hide in the green, our eyes on a prize,
Laughing at shadows like clever spies.
With secrets kept close, our hearts in a whirl,
Life's silly adventures, a miraculous whirl.

Sun-Kissed Tranquility

Sunlight spills like lemonade,
Bees buzzing in a lovely parade.
Wobbly chairs, laughter rings,
Chasing dreams on buttered wings.

Wobbly tables hold our treats,
Lemons dance to happy beats.
Sipping joy on summer's breath,
While ants plot a tiny theft.

Mismatched socks, a silly run,
Hilarious tales under the sun.
Orange peels in frisky fights,
As citrus dreams fill warm nights.

Laughter echoes in the air,
Playful winds tousle our hair.
With each giggle, joy does flow,
In our sun-kissed world aglow.

Journeys Among the Fragrant Boughs

Under canopies of sweet delight,
We embark on journeys bright.
Chasing shadows, quick and sly,
With sticky fingers, oh my, oh my!

Each step leads to fruity mirth,
Exploring every patch of earth.
Riddles shared on branches high,
As the giggles chase the sky.

Map in hand, we stray so far,
Finding treasures, a candy jar.
Mischievous squirrels plot and scheme,
As kids giggle and dance, it seems.

In this land of fragrant dreams,
We laugh till nothing's as it seems.
Each hour a splash of bright surprise,
Underneath those crafty skies.

Forgotten Tales of the Orchard

Gather 'round, oh friends of mine,
For tales of mischief, sweet and fine.
A squirrel stole my lunch last week,
Now every dusk he's full of cheek.

Whispers float on zesty breeze,
Of secret dates with bumblebees.
A runaway lemon chase, I swear,
Naught but giggles filled the air.

Grandma's stories, wild and tall,
Of fruit fights, sticky and sprawl.
Lemonade launched from garden chairs,
And all the laughs that fill our snares.

With every tale, the laughter blooms,
In the midst of playful glooms.
Forgotten joys, we weave with glee,
In our sweet orchard, wild and free.

The Symphony of Rustling Leaves

Listen close, the leaves converse,
Telling tales of fun, not a curse.
A symphony of giggles heard,
From sprites of citrus, ever stirred.

Whirling dervishes in the dirt,
Entering contests with laughter's spurt.
Waltzing to the crickets' tune,
Dancing under a gleeful moon.

Rustling leaves reveal our plots,
A gathering of jolly spots.
Fragrant whispers, mischief near,
While silly songs tickle the ear.

So play a note in this lively scene,
Join us where evergreen is keen.
For every rustle, a chuckle springs,
In our symphony, joy reigns and sings.

In the Midst of Tangy Fragrance

In the garden, the fruit did sway,
Lemonade dreams danced in the fray.
A squirrel in shades, so chic and bold,
Nibbled on snacks, as stories unfold.

A cat in a hat, with saucy flair,
Claimed the best spot with utmost care.
While the sun played tricks, the shadows did twirl,
Laughing aloud in a citrusy whirl.

Anecdotes Wrapped in Peel

Jokes on the tree gave a cheerful sound,
As birds wore ties to gather around.
An orange rolled by with a wink and a grin,
Boasting of adventures, oh where to begin!

A parrot squawked tales of peels so bright,
Fleeting tales shared in the fading light.
Each chuckle was juicy, a fruity surprise,
As laughter spilled forth from all of our eyes.

Twilight Beneath the Boughs

In twilight's glow, a picnic unfurled,
With sandwiches stacked and laughter swirled.
A raccoon arrived with a grin far too wide,
Claiming the snacks, trying to hide!

The fireflies blinked in a winking dance,
While squirrels debated the best costume chance.
Under the stars, the antics did rise,
With mirth in the air, a feast for the eyes.

The Dance of Blossoms and Bees

Blossoms were twirling like they were in fame,
While bees donned shades for their dance of acclaim.
One flower waltzed with a bumblebee bold,
Spinning in circles, a sight to behold!

A frisbee flew by, missed by a bee,
Who buzzed in a circle, quite fancily.
In this fragrant ballet, the laughter took flight,
With petals and pollen, they swayed through the night.

Berry-Laden Wishes and Hopes

Underneath the berry bowls,
A squirrel steals a snack from rolls.
He giggles as he scurries fast,
Dreaming of his berry feast that lasts.

The birds all chirp and laugh aloud,
While trees sway nicely, tall and proud.
They whisper tales of tasty treats,
And dance around on tiny feet.

Old Mr. Buzzy bumbles by,
Tripping on a berry pie.
With jelly on his wobbly nose,
He grins and claims it's art, who knows?

The sun beams down in sheer delight,
As creatures play in pure moonlight.
Hope springs forth from those tiny seeds,
With berry-laden, chuckled leads.

A Canopy of Whispers and Secrets

In shadows deep, the secrets throng,
A parrot cracks his jokes all day long.
The branches whisper and peek down low,
While rabbits giggle with a wink and a bow.

A wise old owl starts to snore,
While sneaky raccoons plot and explore.
They swipe the snacks left out too late,
And run away with light-hearted fate.

The breeze hums songs of past delights,
As fireflies dance through starry nights.
Beneath the rustling leaf confetti,
Everyone twirls, feeling all petty.

Promises hang like ripe, strange fruit,
As tales unravel, shy and cute.
Each giggle ripples through the air,
A canopy filled with whimsy and flair.

Threads of Gold in Green Canopies

Among the leaves, the sunlight weaves,
Golden threads through swaying eaves.
The spiders spin with crafty grins,
On leafy lanes where mischief begins.

Chipmunks share their silly tales,
In acorn caps like tiny sails.
They launch their dreams up to the sky,
With a bounce, a giggle, then whoosh! They fly!

Old Tilly Toad takes a deep dive,
In puddles where all the critters thrive.
With splashes bright, she starts her show,
Making all the flowers grow!

So come and join the merry crew,
With laughter thick as morning dew.
In this garden, fun's the rule,
Where nature plays the jester's fool.

Timeless Tales in Citrus Groves

In groves where citrus scents collide,
A sneaky fox begins to glide.
He tells the tales of silly sins,
And dances lightly; oh, the grins!

A lemon drops his tart surprise,
While orange laughs with sunny eyes.
The grapefruit rolls and joins the game,
Citrus friends, they're all quite the same!

The bees buzz softly, gossiping joy,
While hedgehogs play and nudge the toys.
They chat about the fruit they stole,
Creating laughter as the squirrels stroll.

Under the branches, stories thrive,
With every giggle feeling alive.
These timeless plots in sweet sunshine,
Remind us all how fun can shine.

Enchanted Shadows of Sweetness

In the garden where fruit smiles,
A squirrel juggles for a while.
Chasing shadows, what a sight,
He stumbles, takes a silly flight.

Lemons laugh from high above,
Citrus teasing, full of love.
With every breeze, they whisper jokes,
While giggling hard, they call the folks.

Bees in bow ties buzz at play,
Dancing round, they steal the day.
Orange slices on a plate,
But watch out! They just might skate.

Laughter rolls like juice so sweet,
As mischief leaves a sticky treat.
Under branches full of cheer,
It's a party, spread the beer!

The Legacy of Radiant Harvests

A family feast with fruits galore,
Grandpa claims the juiciest score.
A grandchild's hand slips in the pie,
A splatter of peach makes grandma cry!

Citrus balls roll across the floor,
Dodging feet that bump and soar.
Kids giggle while they leap and climb,
Orange juice fights, oh, what a crime!

A cat in shades and a sun hat too,
Chasing dreams of the fruity brew.
Harvest time becomes a spree,
With our laughter, can't you see?

Hopeful harvests filled with fun,
The shenanigans have just begun.
With bright hues that steal the show,
Every moment, brings a glow!

Whispers of Sunlit Canopies

Under a sky so bright and bold,
Lemonade dreams begin to unfold.
A parrot mimics grandpa's sigh,
As he slips on a peel and flies!

Sunlight dances through the leaves,
While sneaky squirrels plot their thieves.
The chatter of laughter fills the air,
As kids search for a fruity affair.

Citrus balloons float up so high,
Each one's a plan to touch the sky.
But hold on tight, don't let them fly,
They might just sprout wings and say goodbye!

In a world of zesty cheer,
Sweetness lives in every sphere.
With giggles shared beneath the light,
Our jokes and sunshine take their flight!

Shadows of Citrus Dreams

In a realm where laughter grows,
Oranges tell their funny woes.
'Why did the fruit cross the lane?'
To dodge a pie that had a stain!

Under lemons, shadows prance,
Dancing around in a citrus dance.
A bear in shades enjoys the fun,
Sipping juice in the glowing sun.

Kids laugh hard, their faces bright,
As oranges plot their buggy flight.
The garden bursts with zest and cheer,
Creating memories year by year.

At twilight, the jokes still buzz,
A world of whimsy, just because.
These happy shadows, dreamlike streams,
Are made of laughter and citrus dreams!

Whispers of Citrus Breezes

In sunlit glades, the squirrels play,
Chasing shadows, laughing all day.
The tangy scent fills the air,
While bees hum tunes, a buzzing affair.

Lemons roll like tiny balls,
As them tumble, the laughter calls.
A parrot drops a witty line,
As oranges dance, oh how they shine!

A merry breeze sways branches tight,
Tickling all in pure delight.
The sun winks in leafy shade,
While playful pranks in fruit parade.

With every slip, a giggle grows,
As citrus whirls and mischief flows.
In this orchard, joy takes flight,
Where every citrus has a bite!

Shadows in the Sunlit Orchard

In the shade, the shadows play,
An otter jokes, it's quite the display.
A lizard slips on its shiny scale,
As giggles echo with each little tale.

Around the trunk, the raccoons prance,
Throwing fruit as they dance.
One slips down, with a startled yelp,
While others chuckle, no help to help!

Citrus smirks from every branch,
As squirrels plan their daring chance.
With each miss, big bursts of cheer,
They won't stop until spring is near.

In this realm where shadows weave,
Funny things, it's hard to believe.
The laughter rings, a joyful tune,
As day turns bright into the moon.

The Secrets of Sun-Kissed Leaves

The leaves whisper jokes in breezy tones,
As critters clamor with silly groans.
A parrot squawks, 'Tell me a tale!'
And laughter erupts like a breezy gale.

The oranges share with fruits so bright,
A secret recipe for pure delight.
With each peel, a giggle slips,
As sweet juice runs from bouncing lips.

The lemons smirk as they twirl round,
Emerging from shadows with giddy sound.
A game of tag with little bugs,
As laughter blooms in buzzing hugs.

So gather close, the orchard calls,
For fun awaits as sunlight falls.
In this realm where secrets sprout,
Joy is the theme, without a doubt!

Nectar Dreams and Branches Sway

In dreamy lands where nectar flows,
Silly bees wear tiny clothes.
They flit about, so full of glee,
Buzzing tunes, a bumblebee spree.

The branches sway, a dance unique,
While ladybugs play hide and seek.
One gets caught, what a loud fuss!
As friends laugh hard, there's no need to rush.

Under the sun, laughter ignites,
Where citrus mischief sparks delights.
Each twist, each turn, a comic scene,
In this orchard, laughter is supreme!

When the day ends and stars appear,
The blossoms hum with evening cheer.
In nectar dreams, our hearts will stay,
As branches sway through night and day!

The Alluring Dance of Shadows

In a grove where shadows prance,
Lemons wear a quirky stance.
Sunbeams tickle leaves with glee,
Dancing squirrels join the spree.

A monkey thinks he's quite the star,
Steals the fruit, oh, what a czar!
He juggles oranges in the air,
With every slip, we all just stare.

Grasshoppers hum a funny song,
While a cat tries to tag along.
But every leap ends in a fail,
As she lands right on the trail.

Amidst the laughter, blooms still sway,
In this charming, silly play.
Nature's jesters, what a sight,
In the sunlight, pure delight!

Sun-Soaked Lullabies and Tales

A nap under the sun, I take,
Where dreams of juice and zest awake.
Midday snoozes filled with joy,
Even dreams can be a ploy.

A lizard croons a little tune,
To woo a frog beneath the moon.
They croak and chirp, a funny sight,
A nighttime jam that feels just right.

The bees bring laughter with their buzz,
While flowers giggle, just because.
A butterfly in socks so bright,
Makes the garden feel just right.

Underneath the sunny rays,
Silly stories, happy days.
With each tickle from the breeze,
The world's a stage, laugh as you please!

Fragments of Citrus Light

In a patch of citrus dreams,
Rabbits scheme and plot their schemes.
They toss sweet peels like confetti,
Making every creature ready.

A sprite holds court, a jester keen,
Juggling fruits like a circus scene.
With every tumble, giggles swell,
What a great, enchanting spell!

Ants parade with fruit hats bold,
Strutting past the marigold.
Their tiny feet tap from the sun,
Turning chores into pure fun.

Glimmers dance on lemon's skin,
Silly laughter draws you in.
Nature's jesters, oh so bright,
Playing games in golden light!

The Harvest's Silent Witness

The harvest moon begins to grin,
Watching critters race and spin.
With chuckles soft and pitter-pat,
A raccoon wears a giant hat.

The farmer trips on scattered grain,
While the scarecrow offers refrain.
Straw-stuffed laughter fills the air,
As dancing crows, they do declare.

In baskets, fruits make quite a scene,
As giggles echo, sweet and keen.
Each slice of pie brings cheers galore,
Thankful for the harvest score.

While fireflies join the evening glow,
Nature's workers steal the show.
And in this fun-filled, silly fest,
The night becomes the very best!

Beneath the Swaying Canopy

Swaying limbs dance with glee,
Fruits debating who's the best,
Lemons roll with a cheeky grin,
While oranges play a game of jest.

Squirrels gather for a feast,
Chasing ants, what a sight,
Banana peels become their slides,
In their tree-top delight.

A bird joins in with a tune,
Mocking the fruits with a caw,
It's a party up in the branches,
Nature's own little circus law.

Who knew a day in the sun,
Could spark such silly fun?
With laughter and fruit confetti,
May this wacky joy be never done!

A Harvest of Light and Shadow

A light breeze whispers a joke,
As shadows swing to and fro,
Citrus laughs in sunny tones,
And throws a comedy show.

Lemons wearing silly hats,
Followed by a line of limes,
They invite the oranges, too,
To compete in fruity rhymes.

Little ants in tiny cars,
Zooming on their leafy pace,
Each stop a break for snacks to munch,
While the sun laughs in its place.

Under fluttering leaves we sit,
Snickering at the fun they weave,
Who knew trees could tell such tales?
Just wait, there's more up their sleeve!

Echoes of Rustling Leaves

In the rustle there's a giggle,
A babble of whispers from above,
Silly tales of fruity things,
A zesty maze of quirky love.

Leaves gossip about a squirrel,
Who thinks he's king of the tree,
But oranges roll their eyes with flair,
Declaring, "He's just nutty!"

A dance-off breaks the stillness,
As the fruits sway in delight,
Each one tries to out-funk the other,
In their vibrant, fruity fight.

Echoing laughter fills the air,
Beneath this leafy disguise,
Nature's comedy show reigns true,
With every sway, another surprise!

Citrus Promises in the Breeze

The breeze blows in with a chuckle,
Promising zesty delight,
Citrus giggles on branches high,
Under the warm, sunny light.

An orange winks at a passersby,
Saying, "Come join in our fun!"
While lemons plan a daring heist,
To steal the sun when it's done.

A parrot squawks a cheeky pun,
As squirrels tumble in the shade,
It's a circus of fruity mirth,
In this canopy parade.

And as shadows stretch and yawn,
The fruits wave their last goodbyes,
Tomorrow's laughter awaits anew,
In nature's grand enterprise.

A Tapestry of Citrus Hues

In groves where oranges gleam bright,
Squirrels dance in sheer delight.
A fruit falls down, goes duly splat,
And on the ground, a startled cat.

Bees buzz by in quite the flurry,
With nectar sweet, they seem to hurry.
A clownish duck steals all the show,
Waddling fast, then moving slow.

Leaves rustle, secrets dare to play,
A monkey swings and shouts hooray!
He juggles fruits with utmost flair,
As laughter bounces through the air.

In twilight's glow, all joins the fun,
A citrus party has begun.
With zest and joy, we sing aloud,
In nature's blend, we are so proud.

Laughter Echoes in Glistening Groves

A parrot tells the funniest tale,
Of kids who tried to ride a snail.
Their giggles mix with leaves that sway,
While ants march on in strict array.

A worm in stripes thinks he looks grand,
But slips and lands right in the sand.
The birds all chuckle, wings a-flap,
As nature beams, not one mishap.

A toad croaks jokes, a real delight,
Though frogs just roll their eyes in spite.
With splashes, jumps, and silly plays,
The funniest of summer days.

In bright green patches, joy unceasing,
Each creature's wish, a laughter releasing.
A melody of chuckles merge,
In citrus realms, the fun's a surge.

Secrets Held in Twigs and Fruit

In secret nooks, a treasure found,
A squirrel's stash of snacks around.
He twitches nose, then takes a bite,
As all his pals join in the bite.

A lemon whispers tales of glee,
Of dapper ants who dance with spree.
While bees gossip about the breeze,
And share the juiciest of teas.

Twigs twist tightly, dreams enclose,
A hidden dance in leafy clothes.
Amidst the fruits, shenanigans fly,
As laughter echoes, oh my, oh my!

The scurrying feet, a playful scene,
In that warm patch of vibrant green.
All join together for a chat,
While secrets hide where tails are fat.

Sun-Warmed Stories of the Earth

Under sunny skies, the tales unfold,
Of fruit that whispered brave and bold.
A pickle in the orange glow,
Tried to tell jokes, but was too slow.

A lizard in a sun hat beams,
While dancing in the golden dreams.
With every hop, a giggle bursts,
The joy of summer, it just thirsts.

An orange fox, with quite the grin,
Brought all his friends, let fun begin.
Citrusy laughter filled the air,
As silly antics filled our care.

In warm embrace of nature's cheer,
Every creature draws so near.
Together we share a sunny worth,
In stories sprouted from the earth.

A Tangle of Light and Leaf

In the branches, squirrels dance,
Chasing shadows, taking a chance.
A sudden thud, they tumble down,
With acorns raining all around.

Laughter rings from buzzing bees,
Stinging jokes, oh please, oh please!
A jam of colors, green and bright,
Mistaken for a fashion night.

A picnic spreads, sandwiches flop,
Ants quite eager for a swap.
Slip on a crust, oh what a sight,
Nature's clowns in broad daylight!

The sun peeks through, a golden eye,
Casting giggles in the sky.
Where folks relax, and life's a breeze,
Savoring fresh-cut leafy cheese.

Where Nature's Stories Unfold

A tale begins with rustling leaves,
Each whisper tickles, each giggle weaves.
A frog in glasses reads a book,
While passersby can't help but look.

The wind chuckles, what a tease,
Turning pages with such ease.
A hawk debates, perched on a snag,
Should he swoop or just wag?

The flowers gossip, colors bright,
Claiming who's the biggest fright.
"Oh please," blushes blooming thyme,
"Just because I smell divine!"

As laughter fills the sunlit glade,
Time slows down, fun never fades.
Grab a seat on nature's floor,
Stories abound, so much in store!

Fragrant Footsteps in the Shade

Skip along the grassy lane,
In the shade, we'll play the game.
Each step releases fragrant snorts,
Who smells best? Our floral ports!

A runaway hat on a gusty breeze,
Chased by giggles, swaying trees.
The world's a stage, so why not twirl?
Dance with daisies, give them a whirl!

Lemonade spills on the ground,
Splashing joy, all around.
"Who ordered sunshine with a twist?"
Mangoes sigh, "We won't be missed!"

Jokes amongst crickets in the night,
With every chirp, a new delight.
To have such friends of feathered cheer,
Makes every moment bright and clear.

An Ode to the Sunlit Grove

Here in this cozy sunlit space,
Nature's laughter wears a face.
A chipmunk prances, socks askew,
Dramatic flair like actors do!

Bouncing on branches, a wise old crow,
Crows the news, puts on a show.
The sunlight filters, casting spots,
Where giggles dance and laughter knots.

Beside the brook, a frog sings loud,
Caterpillars shimmy, forming a crowd.
"I'm a butterfly!" one claims with glee,
"Watch out, folks, no bug can flee!"

With every bloom and every sound,
Joyful moments in nature found.
An ode to fun, where humor thrives,
In sunlit groves, our spirit jives!

Beneath a Canopy of Gold

In the shade where laughter grew,
Bouncing fruits sang a tune or two.
A squirrel danced, with nuts in tow,
Declaring himself the king of show.

Chasing shadows, slipping past,
A bee hums loud, but moves so fast.
Footprints laugh upon the ground,
As nature's mischief spins around.

Under golden hues that gleam,
A pup leaps high, it's quite the scene.
Tail wagging, he claims his prize,
An orange roll—what a surprise!

Friends gathering for a game,
Silly faces, none the same.
Each fruit a trophy, none too sweet,
But giggles ensure a grand retreat.

Serenade of the Swaying Limbs

Branches sway, a rhythm true,
Barking dogs join in the cue.
A bird in shades of bright and bold,
Decides to sing of tales untold.

A gentle breeze holds secrets tight,
While critters join the lively fight.
Each swing and sway tells stories shared,
Of sunny pranks that none have dared.

The sun peeks in with winking eyes,
IT snickers at the so-called wise.
A couple trips on roots so sly,
As laughter rings and worries fly.

In harmony, the leaves approve,
Nature's whim maintains the groove.
A merry jest from branch to bough,
In this serene and silly row.

In the Heart of the Harvest

Gather 'round, let's share a cheer,
For all the bounty that draws near.
With dancing feet and faces bright,
Fruits smile back in pure delight.

Jars of jam and pies galore,
Sticky fingers on the floor.
Kids take swings at the hanging fare,
Orange splats caught in the air!

Giggling ants share little bites,
While butterflies take scenic flights.
The harvest talks to passersby,
With fruity jokes that make us cry.

Each fruit a jester, bright and round,
Fooling all, then tumbling down.
In the heart of cheer and light,
Lies a harvest pure delight.

Sunlit Reflections in the Green

Sunshine winks, the leaves reply,
With whispers soft like lullabies.
A pair of shades rests on the ground,
Awaiting laughter, joy unbound.

The grass tickles each foot as it creeps,
While ladybugs play hide and seek leaps.
A quirky hat finds its way too,
Declared as fashion—what a view!

Beneath the gaze of skies so blue,
Pups chase shadows, funny, true.
Unruly ants parade in line,
Marching to a sunny design.

With a splash of color, the day unfolds,
In every giggle, a tale retold.
With every glance, the world's a scene,
Of sunlit pranks in vibrant green.

Dreams Cradled Amongst the Boughs

In the shade of citrus cheer,
A squirrel shimmies, full of beer.
With acorns laced in dreamy bliss,
Who knew squirrels could dance like this?

The branches giggle, swaying low,
Tickling dreams that like to glow.
Lemons laugh, they roll and tease,
While bees don sunglasses with great ease.

A rabbit hops, a silly prance,
Chasing shadows in a trance.
The fruit is ripe, the jokes are old,
But laughter here is purest gold.

Underneath the vibrant leaves,
The world spins as the sunlight weaves.
Who knew nature could be so wise,
With nutty tricks and funny skies?

The Symphony of Blooming Life

A chorus of crickets starts to croon,
While daisies sway to a silly tune.
Butterflies bust out in a dance,
Even cacti join the chance!

The worms are wiggling, quite a show,
Learning steps in a rowdy row.
Grasshoppers leap, with a chirpy cheer,
"Who knew spring had such flair this year?"

The flowers flirt with buzzing bees,
Trading nectar for laughs with ease.
Bees in bow ties, they flit and zoom,
In this concert held beneath the bloom.

As raindrops join the swirling fun,
The puddles reflect a giggling sun.
Life blooms wild, with humor rife,
Who wouldn't want this blooming life?

Treading Softly on Sunlit Paths

Where sunbeams dance upon the ground,
A toddler skips without a sound.
With sticky hands and chocolate trails,
She leads the squirrels on laughter sails.

A dog spins round, chasing his tail,
While ants march on, a tiny trail.
Sunshine drips on blooms so bright,
As giggles echo through the light.

Together here, in joyful play,
The world feels fresh, a bright bouquet.
With each soft step, the earth will hum,
Join in the fun, it's time to come!

The path is lined with vibrant glee,
With every step, we're wild and free.
Oh, what a joy to roam and laugh,
On these sunlit paths, we find our craft!

The Colors of Forgotten Sunsets

The sky explodes in orange hues,
Like fruit punch spilled on worn-out shoes.
Clouds brush the air with goofy flair,
Winking at stars that giggle, "Where?"

The horizon yawns with sleepy giggles,
As evening waltzes with playful wiggles.
A raccoon dons a wide-brimmed hat,
And gives a nod to the old chitchat.

Fireflies twinkle with silly glee,
Whispering secrets to the breeze, you see.
In colors bright, the day says bye,
With a wink and a flip, off to the sky!

So let us laugh at the day's sunset,
With hues that play, we won't forget.
In this light, our spirits soar,
As we twirl in colors forevermore.

Echoes from the Leafy Depths

In shadows deep where laughter sings,
The squirrels practice acrobatic flings.
An owl in glasses reads a book,
While frogs in ties just dance and crook.

The air is thick with citrus zest,
As mice in tuxes take their rest.
A rabbit juggles fruit with flair,
While crickets croon a lively air.

A tortoise drags a heavy case,
Claiming it's his time and space.
With every step, he drops a snack,
As birds all cheer, "Come, let's unpack!"

In these heights, joy takes a whirl,
Where yo-yos fly and tails unfurl.
The moon and sun play hide and seek,
While giggles echo, soft yet sleek.

The Hummingbird's Lullaby

With wings all fluttery and small,
A hummingbird prepares to call.
She finds a flower just for kicks,
And winks at bees to share her tricks.

A beetle dressed in dapper wear,
Bows low before the flower fair.
As nectar spills and giggles grow,
A party's planned for all below.

The ants bring snacks of crumbly cake,
The roaches join, for friendship's sake.
They dance on petals, stomp and sway,
Creating joy in wild ballet.

They toast to petals, sweet and bright,
As evening brings the cozy night.
With laughter ringing in the air,
The tiny guests forget their care.

Secrets in the Citrus Shade

In dappled light, where shadows play,
The chatter grows, come what may.
A lizard dives in splashes quick,
While breezes tease, like laughter's trick.

Beneath the leaves, a meeting's set,
The garden's gossips seldom fret.
A turtle shares a tale of woe,
While all his friends just gawk and go.

The fruit hangs low, a citrus feast,
As critters dance, both west and east.
Bats flying low, their shadows glint,
While limes roll down without a hint.

Amid this tale of trees and fun,
The day slips by, they've just begun.
With laughter, games, and tasty zest,
In hidden worlds, they find their best.

A Tapestry of Tangy Hues

In hues so bright, the fruit does gleam,
A playful space, just like a dream.
A parrot spins on branches high,
While giggles greet the starlit sky.

With squishy fruit, the squirrels plot,
To make a stew that's hit or not.
A tease of lime, a spritz of cheer,
Their kitchen whirls, "Come taste our dear!"

A hedgehog dons a chef's tall hat,
Preparing feasts that welcome that.
The punchline's missed when fruit flies by,
As everyone lets out a cry.

In tangy glory, they rejoice,
Each critter sings with lively voice.
From dusk till dawn, the laughter rings,
Creating joy on fruity wings.

Where the Marigolds Embrace

In a garden bright and bold,
Marigolds tell stories untold.
Bees dance and buzz, quite the sight,
While ants march on, full of delight.

A squirrel steals seeds without a care,
Chasing shadows, a furry dare.
With petals gold and laughter free,
Nature's jesters, wild and zesty.

Sunbeams tickle the ground below,
Joy blooming where laughter flows.
As butterflies flutter, wings in spree,
The flowers giggle, "Join the jubilee!"

Underneath the sunny cheer,
Funny faces seem to appear.
In this patch, no one feels blue,
With marigolds laughing, it's all true!

Daylight's Golden Canopy

Up above the leaves applaud,
As sunlight drips and flaws are flawed.
A cat in shade, with a lazy yawn,
Dreams of fish till the break of dawn.

The breeze plays tricks, like a cheeky sprite,
Tickling toes with pure delight.
A picnic spread, ants crashing the show,
With crumbs and giggles that overflow.

Clouds drift by, a fluffy parade,
While shadow puppets dance in the glade.
A squirrel wearing shades, oh what a sight,
Sipping on dew, living the light!

When laughter rings, the day's complete,
In this golden shade, all hearts meet.
So grab your friends, the day's still young,
Under bright skies, let's sing and have fun!

Under the Scent of Blossoms

In the air, sweet perfume wafts,
Bees on a break, sipping on drafts.
A dog in daisies, howling tunes,
While the sun just snores in afternoon.

Petals drop like confetti, oh dear!
It's a party thrown by the flowers here.
With candy-colored blooms, a vibrant spree,
Laughter echoes as wild as can be.

A butterfly stumbles, mid-flight glide,
On a snicker of breeze, it takes a slide.
Grasshoppers chuckle with leaps and bounds,
As we dance in circles, spinning round.

In this fragrant realm, let joy overflow,
Pollen confetti, a bright yellow glow.
So come and join this blissful charade,
With blossoms laughing, we'll never fade!

Entwined in Autumn's Glow

Crimson leaves spin down like a dance,
Making way for the squirrels' romance.
With each rustle, a giggle's shared,
As acorns tumble, carelessly bared.

A crow in a sweater, quite the sight,
Preening feathers in the warm sunlight.
Pumpkin pies cooling on window sills,
While children embrace fall's joyful thrills.

The winds do cartwheels, leaves in tow,
Chasing laughter wherever they go.
Hot cocoa sips, we toast with cheer,
In cozy corners, all hearts draw near.

As twilight dips in a blush so bright,
Autumn winks, "Let's party tonight!"
So gather 'round, let's make a meme,
In nature's book, we'll write our dream!

Gentle Breezes and Citrus Sighs

The wind sings loud, a playful tune,
While lemons giggle, quite the funny boon.
Limes roll around, they play peek-a-boo,
In the shade of branches, what a silly view!

Squirrels dance, their tails like ribbons,
Searching for snacks, while no one's given.
A parrot squawks, he wants a lime slice,
And claims it's better than plain old rice.

Frogs jump high, donning citrus hats,
Debating over which one's got the best stats.
And bees buzz loud, in quite the ruckus,
Mixing up nectar in a fruity circus!

So let us join this zesty affair,
Sharing laughs, without a single care.
With every giggle, another fruit drops,
In this merry orchard, joy never stops!

The Lure of Tangy Whispers

A zestful breeze flirts with our hats,
As oranges tease, like playful chats.
Tasting the sun, with a cheeky grin,
What's sweeter than sweetness, let's begin!

A careless squirrel slips on a peel,
While we all burst out, it's the best kind of reel.
Citrus laughter echoes around,
In this sunny spot, pure joy is found!

The flowers join in, with colors so bright,
Dancing with bees, oh what a delight!
Beneath the branches, we all find a place,
Underneath the gold, with a splash of grace.

So gather 'round, let the jests commence,
In this funny realm, laughter's immense.
For in every fruit, there's a giggle or two,
Join in the fun, we're waiting for you!

Reflections of the Golden Hour

As dusk arrives, the laughter grows,
Citrus dreams dance with silly prose.
Shadows stretch with a skip and a hop,
While oranges chuckle, they never stop!

Frolicking critters in leafy attire,
Each fruit gets a shot at a stand-up flyer.
Sugar-coated smiles under the sun,
Find the wittiest one, oh what fun!

We raise our cups filled with juice so bright,
Toasting to friends and the silly moonlight.
Under the hues of orange and gold,
Every tale shared turns more bold.

So sit back, relax, let the jokes unfurl,
With citrus companions, let our laughter swirl.
The golden hour shines with glee,
As we gather 'round, oh joyously free!

The Poetry of Sun-Drenched Life

Under the sun, where mischief waits,
Limes hold a contest, debating their fate.
Lemonade stands, with signs all aglow,
Quenching our thirst in a comical show!

A squirrel in shades makes a bold move,
To steal a sweet treat, he's in the groove!
He slips, he slides, a real juggling act,
While we laugh loud, can't keep it intact!

The playful breeze gives a citrusy tease,
And tickles our nose with such gentle ease.
As giggles erupt from the grove's lively heart,
Every silly moment is a true work of art!

So let us write, with joy in our pen,
Of fruits and fun, as we celebrate again.
With a nod and a wink, under skies so blue,
Life's sweet poetry, just waiting for you!

The Dappled Grove's Secret

In the shade where squirrels plot,
They gather acorns—what a lot!
With cheeks so full, they giggle loud,
In this crazy, nutty crowd.

A rabbit hops and tells a tale,
Of a turtle who tried to sail.
But oh, the boat was just a leaf,
He paddled hard, but faced a reef.

A fox appears, with sly, sharp eyes,
He spins his yarns and spins some fries.
The trees all chuckle, branches sway,
As laughter bubbles through the day.

With whispers sweet, the sunlight glows,
In this grove, anything goes!
A secret place for all to blend,
Where every twist is just a friend.

Moonlit Nectar and Twilight Leaves

The fireflies dance with a ping and a pop,
While fruit bats swoop and never stop.
They wear tiny hats, quite the odd sight,
Playing tag with the stars, oh what a night!

From blossoms sweet, the buzzards hum,
While grumpy frogs play their drum.
A symphony of croaks and tunes,
Underneath the smiling moons.

A mischievous breeze shakes the boughs,
With a wink, it chuckles—oh, the hows!
As the leaves erupt in giggling fits,
Making sure no one ever quits.

Around the glade, the shadows prance,
In nature's merry moonlit dance.
So here we stay, for it's quite clear,
Laughter's sweeter than any beer!

Ciphers of the Gnarled Branches

In ancient limbs, where secrets lie,
Trees gossip softly—oh my, oh my!
They hold the whispers of all who roam,
From cheeky chameleons to birds who comb.

The wise old owl hoots a riddle or two,
While chipmunks giggle, "Who's smarter—me or you?"
They wager nuts and tease with glee,
In this leafy court of absurdity.

Creepy crawlers write their tales,
In ink of sap, on barked sales.
With each scratch, stories come alive,
Of snoozing bears and bees who jive.

Unraveled tales of branches bent,
With every leaf, a new comment.
A kingdom where oddities blend,
And laughter is the best trend.

Where Sunset Colors Dance

When the sun dips low, the colors flare,
The fireflies sparkle like golden hair.
With a wink and giggle, the day takes a bow,
As night comes creeping, swinging its brow.

The peachy hue invites a parade,
Of owls with glasses, wearing a shade.
They clink their cups, toasting with cheer,
"Another fine day we get to end here!"

Crickets orchestrate a nighttime tune,
While raccoons debate who's the best buffoon.
They juggle acorns, with clumsy flair,
Under twinkling skies, with laughter to share.

In this sunset glow, a party ensues,
Each critter brings something new to muse.
A celebration of silly, bright chance,
In a world where whimsy leads the dance.

Echoes of Brightness and Shade

In a bough of laughter, a squirrel takes flight,
Chasing after sunshine, all day and night.
With acorns as missiles, he showers his friends,
While the lazy raccoon just rolls and pretends.

The shadows do giggle, in the heat of the day,
As the kitten tumbles in leaves, in play.
A parrot's loud chatter breaks the peaceful scene,
Complaining that none stay on the green screen.

From a tree branch above, an owl gives a grin,
"Why take life so serious? Where's the fun in?"
With fruit rolling down, they start to engage,
The antics unfold on the natural stage.

Yet as dusk draws near, they all take a pause,
To rest for a moment, bury worries in claws.
In this realm of folly, joy brightly invades,
Echoes of laughter where silliness cascades.

Reveries in the Leafy Arms

Here in leafy arms, daydreams take a spin,
Where a worm in a bowler is hoping to win.
He dances with ants, in a waltz on the ground,
While a grasshopper judges, feet slack all around.

Bumblebees buzz in a fit of delight,
Planning a picnic under cover of night.
But the fruit flies, they argue over who's queen,
As the grapes laugh out loud, "What a sight to be seen!"

The shadows are thick with whispers of cheer,
While a lizard in shades tries to look sincere.
With nonsense and giggles, the creatures collide,
In a leafy cabaret where no one can hide.

Under the glow of a citrusy moon,
The critters all hum a jazzy old tune.
With reveries swirling, and fun as their charm,
They find joy in life's simple leafy arms.

Where Dreams and Citrus Intertwine

In a twist of oranges, dreams fruitfully flow,
A monkey in pajamas swings high, oh so slow.
He juggles the lemons, advancing in style,
As a turtle on roller skates joins with a smile.

The laughter erupts when a squirrel wears a hat,
While a cactus tries dancing, now how about that?
With citrus confetti all over the ground,
The merriest moments are easily found.

As night time approaches, the critters unite,
An orchestra formed by the stars shining bright.
With jokes in the air, and oranges in hand,
They giggle and dance, such a whimsical band.

So here's to the moments when dreams intertwine,
In a realm full of colors, ever so divine.
With mischief and mirth, let's frolic and play,
In silly pursuits, let us always stay!

Reflections in the Fruit-laden Shadows

In shadows so fruity, the giggles are loud,
As a cat in a bowtie draws quite the crowd.
She thinks she's a star in this zany retreat,
While the ducks in formation march on tiny feet.

The apricots whisper, "What's happening here?"
As a gravelly voice calls, "Come join us, oh dear!"
With antics of squirrels performing ballet,
The reflections of fun dance the worries away.

The moon joins the party with a Cheshire-like grin,
Casting light on the laughter that bubbles within.
With lemons as maracas, the show gets underway,
And the laughter is contagious, much to the dismay!

As the shadows grow long, and the night starts to play,
The critters are tired, but they won't fade away.
In fruit-laden whispers, they plot for the morn,
For tomorrow's pursuit will be freshly reborn.

Reviving the Citrus Chorus

In the grove where fruits hang low,
A squirrel sings, putting on a show.
Orange peels, a slip and slide,
Watch your step, oh what a ride!

Bees buzzing like a lively band,
They dance around, looking quite grand.
Lemonade rivers flow and twist,
Who knew we'd need a citrus assist?

The parrot squawks a joke or two,
"What did the orange say to you?"
They laugh and roll on grassy floors,
Life's zest is cracked, with silly roars!

So grab a wedge and join the fun,
Under the sun, we've just begun.
With citrus bliss, let's share the cheer,
In this grove, there's nothing to fear!

Journeying Through Golden Shadows

In a land of juicy, fruity heights,
We took a trip on sunny flights.
The fruits wore shades with style and class,
Sipping juice from a fancy glass!

We stumbled on a citrus ghost,
He claimed to be the peel king's host.
With laughter ringing through the trees,
He scared us off with zest-filled sneeze!

A rabbit offered us a treat,
"Citrus cake that can't be beat!"
But tripped on oranges, fell with grace,
Spilled juice all over the place!

As we journeyed, smiles did grow,
Golden shadows began to glow.
In this citrus tale grand and bright,
We danced and played through day and night!

An Escape in Sweet Surrender

We fled to where the fruit trees vie,
For space to thrive, oh my oh my!
A hammock strung in tangy bliss,
Fruits above, who could resist?

We plotted wild escape, just so,
Dodging seeds and sunset glow.
With orange juice as our main guide,
In citrus dreams we took our ride!

A twisty path of lime and cheer,
With laughter echoed, loud and clear.
Frogs croaked jokes in silly tone,
This citrus place felt like our own!

In sweet surrender, we found peace,
As every citrus worry ceased.
With friends and fruit, we joined the fun,
In our escape, we truly won!

The Allure of Orchard Memories

In an orchard where the laughter flows,
We gathered stories as the sun glows.
Picnic blankets, wild and bright,
Snacked on fruits 'til the moonlight!

A clever dog steered clear of brambles,
While the kids played silly gambles.
With juice on faces and giggles loud,
We felt like the silliest crowd!

Old old tree told tales of yore,
Of past escapades, laughter galore.
With every gust, secrets unfold,
In every bite, a story told!

In our hearts, these moments stay,
As golden fruit leads the way.
Orchard memories that dance and sway,
A funny feast that won't decay!

The Verses of a Fruitful Dance

In a twist and a twirl with zest,
The lemons wear hats made of rest.
Limes laugh and roll on the ground,
As oranges cheer with a joyful sound.

With peels that slip and slides that spin,
Grapefruits giggle at the playful din.
Dancing so much, the fruits lost their way,
Now they're all stuck in a fruit buffet!

They salsa on leaves and cha-cha on vines,
Rhythms of laughter, the best of times.
But watch your step, or you might get squished,
A fruity folly that's simply delish!

As night falls, the fruit band takes a break,
Chatting of sunshine and sweet kale shake.
In the moonlight, their party resumes,
A citrus celebration that outshines blooms!

Embracing the Citrus Sunset

As day fades, oranges dream in blue,
Their peels glow bright, a radiant hue.
They laugh at the shadows that creep and crawl,
Wishing on lemons when night starts to fall.

Limes throw parties with zest in the air,
While pineapples tumble without any care.
Each squeeze brings a giggle, rushes of cheer,
Mixed drinks for all in the twilight's sphere.

The sun dips low, a custard surprise,
Behind the citrus, it waves its goodbyes.
While grapefruits gossip, their gossip gets loud,
Beneath all the laughter, they feel so proud.

As night approaches, they snicker and sway,
In a chorus of sweetness, they dance and play.
For every sunset holds stories so bright,
In oranges' laughter, we find pure delight!

Cradled in a Citrus Dream

In a hammock of leaves, the fruits take a nap,
With dreams of juicing, they make quite a flap.
Peeling back layers of silly delight,
In tropical whispers, they giggle all night!

Kumquats wiggle in their cozy cocoon,
While tangerines hover, singing their tune.
The zest of their dreams is a flavorful treat,
As they plot fun capers with wriggly feet!

Suddenly, fog rolls in with a squash,
Splattering juice with a loud 'kerplosh!'
The fruits all chuckle and wriggle with glee,
As they bounce in a frenzy, so happy and free.

When dawn breaks, they yawn and stretch tall,
In a citrus realm where best friends enthrall.
In dreams made of laughter, they shan't want to flee,
Cradled in joy, that's the key to be free!

A Secret Life of Leaves

The leaves conspire under a wobbly sun,
Whispering jokes 'til the day is done.
Mint shares out secrets, so fresh and so bold,
While basil grins, loved stories retold.

They wiggle and giggle without any care,
In the company of fruits lounging there.
Persimmons plot their next pranky delight,
While herbs trade their tales, tickling the night.

With every breeze, there's laughter and fun,
As leaves flip and flop, on a daily run.
In the breeze, they dance, a comical sight,
From dawn until dusk and into the night.

So raise up a toast from a leaf like a cup,
To the secret lives where the giggles bubble up!
In this quirky garden, life's absurdity thrives,
Where laughter's the bounty that everyone derives!

www.ingramcontent.com/pod-product-compliance
Lightning Source LLC
Chambersburg PA
CBHW060141230426
43661CB00003B/517